asianbarbecue

by Vicki Liley

PERIPLUS EDITIONS
Singapore • Hong Kong • Indonesia

Contents

All About Asian Barbecue

Cooking over fire is one of the oldest and simplest forms of cooking, and it is an inexpensive means of cooking a variety of foods.

Barbecuing has been a way of life for decades throughout Asia, and street food is a mainstay in many Southeast Asian countries. Snacks of satay chicken, stir-fried noodles, dumplings and pancakes are enjoyed on street corners, under temple canopies, cotton umbrellas, silk awnings and widespreading green trees. It's a brilliant kaleidoscope of noise and vividly contrasting smells. The tastes are intense, hot, sweet, salty and bitter. At many street markets, locals also display an array of locally grown fruit and vegetables along with brightly colored crafts and clothing, all for barter or sale.

This enjoyable alfresco style of eating demands the freshest ingredients and, because these street foods frequently have to be displayed, cooked and sold without refrigeration, the turnover must be rapid and the heat of the cooking intense. The spicing and marinating often contribute to preserving the foods as well as adding flavor. *Asian Barbecue* reflects the flavors and cooking traditions of many Asian countries, including Singapore, Vietnam, Thailand, China and Korea.

There are many varieties of barbecue grills and grill pans. Outdoor and indoor grilling is essentially the same, but outdoor barbecues lend themselves to garden entertaining areas where friends and family can gather while the meal is cooking. Indoor grilling can be done on a tabletop with a Japanese-style hibachi or electric countertop grill, or in a stovetop grill pan in the kitchen—all small by scale to an outdoor barbecue, but still a fast, unique way of cooking with friends and family.

The choice of an outdoor grill or stovetop grill pan will depend on several things, including the number of people you will entertain, the location of the barbecue, storage and the size of the cooking area needed. For example, if the cooking area is too small, the grill will become congested and food won't cook properly. If it's too large, you will waste fuel. Do you want a gas grill that lights automatically, or do you want the challenge of starting a fire? Select a model and type that suits your needs.

Asian-style barbecuing generally requires only a small grill or stovetop grill pan. The Japanese-style hibachi is ideal for Asian-style grilling. Compact, portable, and inexpensive, it is suitable for small balconies and for either indoor or outdoor cooking. It uses charcoal for its heat source. The modern electric countertop grill has a nonstick surface, generally has three or more heat settings and can be opened flat for a larger cooking surface.

Hibachi Grill

Ridged Grill Pan

Stovetop grill pans are available in cast iron or nonstick aluminum and are used on gas or electric stovetops. They are easy to clean and store and are ideal for everyday cooking for up to six people. A well-ventilated kitchen or exhaust hood is recommended for this style of indoor cooking.

The easy-to-use gas grill has multiple heat settings and is available in many sizes and models in all price ranges. Some are connected to a home's gas supply, while others use portable gas bottles or tanks. Kettle grills, heated by charcoal, are available in various lidded sizes, from small up to very large. The smaller models are ideal for Asian barbecuing.

Disposable grills, which use presoaked charcoal briquettes, are inexpensive and require no messy clean up. They must be used on a heatproof rock or brick base and disposed of carefully, once completely cold.

Light-weight portable grills, generally heated with charcoal or wood chips, are simply a smaller version of the backyard grill and are ideal for Asian barbecues anywhere.

Getting started—Starting a gas grill is easy. Open the lid and make sure that the burner controls are off and that there is fuel in the tank or bottle. Turn on the fuel and light the grill according to the manufacturer's instructions. Allow the grill to preheat on high for 10 minutes before cooking.

If you're using a charcoal grill, charcoal briquettes make a good fire and are easy to use. The most common way to start a charcoal fire is to build a pyramid of charcoal on a grate in the fire pan, soak it with the lighter fluid if the briquettes aren't presoaked and carefully light it. Be sure to purchase good quality briquettes, as many of the cheaper brands can impart a chemical flavor to food.

A popular and ecological alternative to using lighter fluid or presoaked briquettes is the charcoal chimney starter, a sheet metal cylinder, available at stores selling barbecue supplies. Place the chimney starter on the barbecue grate, stuff crumpled newspaper in the base, pile charcoal briquettes on top and light the paper. Either way, the coals are ready when they are covered with pale grey ash, generally in about 20 minutes. Carefully distribute the coals from the pyramid or tip them from the chimney starter onto the barbecue grate. You are now ready to start grilling.

For electric countertop grills, plug into the power source, turn on and preheat according to the manufacturer's instructions. For stovetop grill pans, place the clean pan over high heat on the stove and preheat for 5 minutes before cooking. For disposable barbecues, follow the manufacturer's instructions.

Equipment—Long-handled utensils, like tongs, forks, and metal spatulas, are essential for turning foods during cooking. Keep a separate pair of long-handled tongs for moving coals around if need be. Heatproof mitts are also essential for a successful barbecue, and basting brushes and an apron may come in handy.

Controlling the heat—Heat is regulated in a charcoal grill by moving the briquettes with a set of long-handled tongs. Push them closer together to intensify the heat, or spread them apart to cool down the fire. The air vents on the grill provide a similar control. Open them to increase the heat level, or close them to decrease it. On a gas grill, the control dials make it easy to maintain the heat source to suit your cooking. If flames flare up on a gas grill, don't spray with water. The steam can cause burns and can sometimes crack the enamel finish on your barbecue. Instead, close the lid and close the air vents.

Cleaning—Follow manufacturer's instructions for cleaning gas, charcoal and other grills. To clean the cooking grate of a gas grill, turn the burners to high, close the lid and allow it to heat for 5 minutes. Then use a long-handled wire brush to scrape off any food residue. When the grill cools, remove it and clean with hot soapy water. Keep the bottom tray and grease-catch pan clean to prevent fires.

Skewers

Grilled food on skewers has an attractive appeal to cooks and diners alike because of the different flavors, textures and colors that can be cooked and served as one unit. Threading combinations of food onto skewers can also make small quantities of expensive ingredients go a long way.

The foods threaded onto skewers should have the same cooking time, or longer cooking foods, such as potatoes, should be parboiled beforehand. Bamboo skewers need to be soaked in water for 10 minutes before any food is threaded onto them to prevent them from burning.

Both bamboo and stainless steel skewers are available in many sizes. Select the size best suited for the food and the occasion. For example, small cubes of chicken for a party are best threaded onto small bamboo skewers so guests can dispose of the skewers after eating. Unlike bamboo skewers, stainless steel skewers can be cleaned and reused.

Fresh rosemary and bay leaf stems can be used as an attractive and flavorsome alternative to bamboo or stainless steel skewers. However, make sure the stems are woody, not the young soft stems, and soak them in water before use. Lemongrass, sugarcane and bamboo shoots are also sometimes used as skewers for food.

Marinating

One of the easiest ways to add flavor to food before grilling is to marinate it. Foods can be marinated for a few minutes or up to several hours, and even overnight. The longer the marinating time, the stronger the flavor will be, so don't marinate delicately flavored foods like fish for too long. Marinating also enhances the moisture level of the food, keeping it juicy and more succulent after cooking. Leftover marinades can be brushed over the food while it is cooking, or heated and served as a sauce with the cooked meal, but make sure always to boil the marinade for one minute before serving.

Select a mixture of ingredients that complement the food to be marinated. For example, fresh coriander leaves (cilantro) and lime juice complement the subtle flavor of fish and seafood. Remember that strong marinades may sometimes overpower the food itself.

Because many marinades have an acid-based ingredient, like citrus juice or wine, it is best to marinate food in a shallow nonmetallic dish.

Heavy-duty plastic storage bags are also great for marinating foods. Prepared marinades can be stored in screw-top jars in the refrigerator for up to two weeks.

Quick and Easy Marinades

Place any of the following marinade ingredients into a screw-top jar, shake to mix, then brush over food. Cover and refrigerate the food for 10 minutes or more, then drain and grill.

Fish, Seafood and Chicken
(for 2–2$^1/_2$ lbs/1–1$^1/_4$ kg)

2 tablespoons oil
2 tablespoons bottled Thai sweet
  chili sauce
2 tablespoons fresh lemon or lime juice
3 cloves garlic, chopped
1 tablespoon peeled and grated
  fresh ginger
1 tablespoon chopped fresh coriander
  leaves (cilantro)
Salt and freshly ground pepper to taste

Beef, Lamb and Pork
(for 1$^1/_2$–2 lbs/750 g–1 kg)

2 tablespoons oil
1 tablespoon chopped fresh basil leaves
3 tablespoons soy sauce
Grated zest of 1 lemon
3 cloves garlic, chopped
Salt and freshly ground pepper to taste

Vegetables (for 1$^1/_2$–2 lbs/750 g–1 kg)

2 tablespoons oil
2 teaspoons dark sesame oil
2 cloves garlic, chopped
2 teaspoons peeled and grated
  fresh ginger
Salt and freshly ground pepper to taste

Fruit (for 1 lb/500 g)

2 tablespoons fresh lemon or lime juice
1 tablespoon honey
1 teaspoon peeled, grated fresh ginger

Step-by-Step Marinating

1 Prepare the marinade ingredients; mix well.

2 Place the fish, chicken, meat or vegetables into a shallow nonmetallic dish.

3 Brush or pour the marinade over food. Cover and refrigerate for 10 minutes for a light marinade or longer for more pronounced flavors.

4 Drain, then cook on a preheated and oiled gas or charcoal grill or stovetop grill pan to desired doneness.

Quick and Easy Dry Rubs

Dry rubs consisting of breadcrumbs, herbs and spices add flavor and texture to grilled foods. They can also protect food from the harsh heat of the grill, resulting in a more subtle, grilled flavor. A simple coating of breadcrumbs can keep food moist inside while creating a crisp and crunchy outside. Food coated in a blend of fresh herbs and spices can be left to marinate for several hours before cooking. Dry rubs are best used with thinner portions of foods that will cook quickly so the coatings don't burn. Partially cook longer-cooking foods before coating and grilling them. Brush food to be grilled with oil and coat in one of the following dry rub mixtures.

Fish and Seafood (for 2 fish fillets or
steaks)
Grated zest of 1 lemon or lime
2 tablespoons chopped fresh coriander
leaves (cilantro)
1 tablespoon chopped fresh chervil or
parsley
Salt and freshly ground black pepper to
taste

Chicken (for 2 whole chicken breasts)
3 tablespoons fresh white breadcrumbs
1 finger-length red chili pepper,
deseeded and chopped
2 tablespoons chopped fresh basil
leaves
Grated zest of 1 lime
1 clove garlic, minced
Salt and freshly ground black pepper to
taste

Beef, Lamb and Pork (for 2 steaks or
chops)
1 teaspoon five spice powder
1 teaspoon salt
1 teaspoon freshly ground black pepper
2 tablespoons chopped fresh coriander
leaves (cilantro)
1 finger-length red chili pepper,
deseeded and chopped

Step-by-Step Grilling with Rubs

1 Prepare the dry rub ingredients; mix well.

2 Brush fish, chicken, seafood, or meat with oil.

3 Rub the dry seasoning mixture into the surface of the fish, chicken, seafood or meat.

4 Cook on a preheated and oiled grill or stovetop grill pan to desired doneness.

Flavored Butters

A slice of flavored butter placed on a piece of fish, chicken, meat or vegetable hot from the grill forms a warm buttery sauce. Flavored butters are a quick and tasty means of adding additional seasonings. Butters can be made up to 3–4 days ahead of time or frozen for up to 2 months. Flavored butters are rolled into logs, then sliced, scooped or piped onto cooked foods. They are also a delicious spread for warm grilled bread.

Basic Flavored Butter Recipes
In a bowl, mix all ingredients until well
  combined.

Fish and Seafood (1 lb/500 g)

Option 1
$1/_2$ cup (1 stick/125 g) softened butter
Grated zest and juice of 1 lime

Option 2
$1/_2$ cup (1 stick/125 g) softened butter
2 tablespoons chopped fresh coriander
  leaves (cilantro)
1 tablespoon chopped fresh chervil
1 clove garlic, chopped
Juice of 1 lemon

Beef, Lamb and Pork (1 lb/500 g each)

Option 1
$1/_2$ cup (1 stick/125 g) softened butter
2 teaspoons chopped fresh rosemary
1 finger-length red chili pepper, deseeded
  and finely chopped
Freshly ground black pepper to taste

Option 2
$1/_2$ cup (1 stick/125 g) softened butter
2 cloves garlic, chopped
2 green onions (scallions), finely chopped
Freshly ground black pepper to taste

Chicken (1 lb/500 g)

Option 1
$1/_2$ cup (1 stick/125 g) softened butter
2 canned anchovy fillets, drained and
  mashed
Juice of 1 lemon
Freshly ground black pepper to taste

Option 2
$1/_2$ cup (1 stick/125 g) softened butter
2 cloves garlic, finely chopped
1 finger-length green chili pepper, deseeded
  and finely chopped
Grated zest and juice of 1 lime

Step-by-Step Flavored Butters

1 Using a wooden spoon or an electric mixer, beat the butter until soft.

2 Add the flavorings and mix well.

3 Spoon onto a piece of plastic wrap and shape into a log. Roll up and chill until firm.

4 Slice into rounds to serve.

Essential Ingredients

Bean sprouts Sprouting green mung beans are sold either fresh or canned, but the fresh ones tend to have more texture and flavor. Fresh sprouts can be stored in the refrigerator for 2–3 days.

Bok choy A small variety of cabbage with thick white stems and mild-flavored dark green leaves, usually sold 3–4 in a bundle. Chinese broccoli or choy sum can be substituted.

Cracked wheat The whole wheat berry broken into coarse, medium or fine particles. Also called bulghur.

Chili oil Spicy oil produced by steeping dried red chili peppers in oil. Use this hot oil only by the drop. Store in the refrigerator after opening.

Chinese rice wine Low-alcohol Chinese wine, also known as shaoxing wine, made from glutinous rice. Dry sake or dry sherry can be used as a substitute.

Choy sum A Chinese green also known as flowering cabbage. It has yellow flowers, thin stems and a mild flavor and is suitable in most recipes that call for Chinese greens. The entire vegetable (stem, leaves and flowers) is used.

Coconut cream and milk The liquid extracted from grated coconut flesh after soaking in water. Coconut milk is thinner than coconut cream. Used extensively in Thai cooking, it is usually sold in cans.

Dried cellophane noodles Thin translucent noodles made from mung bean starch and sold in bundles. Also called bean thread noodles.

Dried rice vermicelli These noodles are thin round threads made from rice flour and water.

Dried shrimp paste A pungent-flavored paste produced by drying, salting and pounding shrimp, then forming it into blocks or cakes.

Hoisin sauce Sweet, thick Chinese sauce, made from soybeans and also containing vinegar, sugar, chili peppers and other seasonings. Bottled hoisin sauce can be stored indefinitely in the refrigerator.

Hot bean paste A hot, thick red brown sauce made from fermented soybeans, chili peppers, garlic and spices. Sometimes called red bean paste or chili bean paste.

Jasmine rice Aromatic rice, popular in Thai cooking.

Kaffir limes and lime leaves Leaves from the kaffir lime tree are used to add an enticing citrus flavor and aroma to dishes. Dried leaves are readily available, but fresh ones can often be found. Frozen kaffir lime leaves are a good substitute for fresh. Dried leaves are much less flavorful, so use twice as many as the recipe calls for if you're substituting them for fresh leaves. The juice and grated zest of the fruit are also used, but regular lime juice and zest can be substituted.

Fish sauce A pungent sauce of salted, fermented fish and other seasonings, used in sauces, dressings and dipping sauces. Products vary in intensity depending on the country of origin. Fish sauce from Thailand, called *nam pla*, is commonly available. Don't be put off by the strong fishy smell; there is really no substitute.

Five spice powder A classic Chinese spice blend made usually of equal parts ground cinnamon, cloves, fennel seed, star anise and Szechuan peppercorns.

Lemongrass An herb with a long bulbous stalk that has a distinct lemon essence. It is a popular flavoring in Thai and Vietnamese cooking.

Mirin Sweet alcoholic wine made from rice and used in Japanese cooking. Sweet sherry can be substituted.

Oyster sauce A thick, dark brown Chinese sauce made from fermented dried oysters and soy sauce and sold in bottles. It is used to impart an intense or mildly briny flavor to stir-fries and other dishes. Store in the refrigerator after opening.

Palm sugar Dense, heavy, dark cakes of sugar made from the sap of palms trees. Shave with a sharp knife or grate before using. Dark brown sugar can be used as a substitute. Available in Asian markets and many supermarkets.

Sake A clear Japanese wine made from fermented rice.

Soy sauce A salty sauce made from fermented soybeans and usually wheat, and sold in bottles and cans. Available in light and dark varieties; the dark is usually used in cooking and the lighter soy for dipping sauces.

Sesame oil An intensely flavored, dark colored oil made from toasted sesame seeds, sold in bottles, and widely used in Asian cooking. There is no real substitute.

Sesame paste (see Tahini)

Tahini A thick oily paste made from untoasted sesame seeds and traditionally used in Middle Eastern cooking. Asian-style sesame paste is made from toasted sesame seeds, resulting in a paste that is darker in color and more pronounced in flavor than Tahini. Either can be used.

Thai basil Refers to several Asian basil varieties including holy, purple and sweet. Any basil can be used as a substitute.

Thai sweet chili sauce A mild chili sauce with a sweet after taste. Usually used as a dipping sauce, it can also be used on burgers and barbecued meats. Store in the refrigerator after opening.

Wasabi paste A traditional condiment served with Japanese sushi, made from a root similar to horseradish. Available as a paste or in powdered form to be mixed with water.

Wonton wrappers Thin sheets of wheat-based or egg-based dough, square or circular in shape, used to enclose a variety of fillings. Available fresh or frozen. Also called wonton skins or dumpling wrappers.

Spicy Eggplant Dip with Fried Wontons

Served with fried wontons, this delightfully pungent appetizer is an exciting Asian twist on baba ghanoush—a classic roasted eggplant spread with lemon, garlic and tahini. In this recipe grilled eggplant and fresh coriander—a common Asian herb—are a winning flavor combination.

2 medium eggplants, thinly sliced
2 tablespoons olive oil
3 cloves garlic, chopped
$1/_2$ cup (20 g) chopped fresh coriander
  leaves (cilantro)
Juice of 3 lemons
$1/_2$ teaspoon salt or to taste
$1/_2$ teaspoon freshly ground black pepper
$1/_2$ cup (125 ml) tahini or sesame paste

Fried Wonton Wrappers
3 cups (750 ml) oil, for deep frying
36 wonton wrappers

Serves 6–8

1 Brush the eggplant slices with the olive oil. Preheat a grill or stovetop grill pan. Grill the eggplant slices until slightly blackened on both sides, 1–2 minutes each side. Remove from the grill and allow to cool. Place the eggplant, garlic, coriander leaves, lemon juice, salt, pepper and tahini into a food processor and process to a thick paste. Spoon into serving bowls and refrigerate before serving with the Fried Wonton Wrappers.

2 To make the Fried Wonton Wrappers, heat the oil in a large, deep heavy-based saucepan or deep fryer until it reaches 375°F (190°C) or until a small cube of bread dropped in the oil sizzles and turns golden. Working with 2–3 wonton wrappers at a time, deep-fry until golden, about 1–2 minutes. Using a slotted spoon, remove the wonton wrappers from the oil and drain on paper towels.

Grilled Shrimp Salad

Whether eaten chilled or at room temperature when just-tossed, this salad is a great way to enjoy shrimp. The spicy heat of chili peppers and ginger is perfectly balanced with the sweet, cooling flavors of fresh fruit and herbs, creating a sensational flavor-packed appetizer or light meal.

24 fresh jumbo shrimp (king prawns) peeled and deveined, leaving tails intact
2 tablespoons peanut oil
Handful dried cellophane noodles
$1/2$ green papaya, peeled and cut into matchstick lengths
1 mango, peeled and cut into matchstick lengths
1 cup (30 g) loosely packed fresh coriander leaves (cilantro)
$1/2$ cup (15 g) loosely packed fresh basil leaves
$1/4$ cup (25 g) sliced green onions (scallions)

Chili Ginger Dressing
1 finger-length red chili pepper, deseeded and finely chopped
3 tablespoons fish sauce
4 tablespoons fresh lime juice
1 teaspoon dark sesame oil
2 teaspoons peeled and grated fresh ginger
1 teaspoon shaved palm sugar or dark brown sugar

1 Brush the shrimp with the oil. Preheat a grill or stovetop grill pan and grill the shrimp until they change color, 3–4 minutes, turning during cooking. Remove from the grill. Place the noodles in a heatproof bowl, pour in boiling water to cover and allow to stand until the noodles soften, about 10 minutes. Drain and, using scissors, roughly cut the noodles into shorter lengths.
2 To make the Chili Ginger Dressing, place the chili pepper, fish sauce, lime juice, sesame oil, ginger and sugar in a screw-top jar. Shake well to mix.
3 Combine the noodles, shrimp, papaya, mango, coriander, basil and green onions in a mixing bowl. Add the Dressing and toss until well combined. Serve at room temperature or chilled.

Serves 4

Grilled Beef and Mint Summer Rolls

Fresh, crisp and refreshing, these pretty summer rolls are a breeze to make and involve minimal cooking, which is always a plus on hot summer days. Light yet flavorful, summer rolls are a perfect appetizer, whetting your guests' appetites for more to come. They also make a great stand-alone lunch or a snack item.

$3/4$ lb (350 g) boneless sirloin steak
3 cloves garlic, finely chopped
2 teaspoons fish sauce
1 teaspoon dark sesame oil
2 tablespoons oil
$1/3$ cup (80 ml) soy sauce, for dipping

Rolls
3 green onions (scallions), green section only
12 dried rice paper wrappers, $6^{1}/_{2}$ in (15 cm) in diameter
36 large fresh mint leaves
1 English or 3 Japanese cucumbers, cut into matchstick lengths

Makes 12 rolls

1 Place the steak in a shallow nonmetallic dish. In a bowl, combine the garlic, fish sauce and sesame oil. Mix well and brush over the meat. Cover the dish with plastic wrap and refrigerate for 30 minutes. Remove the meat from the marinade.
2 Preheat a grill or stovetop grill pan, then brush the grill surface with the oil. Grill the steak until it is tender, 3–4 minutes each side (beef should remain pink in the center). Remove from the grill, cover with aluminum foil and allow to stand for 5 minutes. Using a sharp knife, slice the steak very thinly.
3 To prepare the Rolls, place the green onions in a saucepan of boiling water for about 15 seconds, or until softened. Then remove and refresh in a bowl of ice water. Cut each scallion lengthwise in 4 pieces.
4 Half fill a bowl with warm water, and place a clean paper towel on your work surface. Dip a rice paper wrapper into the warm water until soft, about 15 seconds, then place it on the paper towel. Place 3 mint leaves and 3 cucumber lengths in the center of the wrapper, top with a small amount of sliced beef and roll up into a cylinder. Tie a scallion length around each roll, then snip off both ends of the roll using scissors.
5 Repeat with the remaining ingredients, covering the prepared rolls with a damp towel to prevent them drying out. Serve with soy sauce.

Note: Dried rice paper wrappers can be found in the dried noodle aisle in Asian markets and natural foods markets.

Spicy Chicken Skewers with Mint Yogurt

Turmeric lends a lovely golden hue to these wonderfully aromatic chicken kebabs. A flavorful marinade imparts a touch of heat that is easily doused with the cooling Cucumber Mint Yogurt.

1^1/$_2$ lbs (750 g) boneless chicken breast
3 teaspoons ground coriander
2 teaspoons ground turmeric
1 finger-length red chili pepper, deseeded
  and finely chopped
4 cloves garlic, finely chopped
2 tablespoons sugar
1 teaspoon salt
12 bamboo skewers
2 tablespoons peanut oil
3 cups (200 g) coarsely chopped choy sum
  or other Asian greens

Cucumber Mint Yogurt
^{1}/$_2$ cup (125 ml) plain yogurt
2 cloves garlic, finely chopped
2 tablespoons chopped fresh mint leaves
^{1}/$_4$ cup (40 g) peeled, deseeded and
  chopped cucumber

1 Cut the chicken into 1^1/$_2$-inch (4-cm) cubes. Combine the ground coriander, turmeric, chili pepper, garlic, sugar and salt in a large bowl. Add the chicken pieces to the bowl and toss to evenly coat with the spice mixture. Cover the bowl with plastic wrap and refrigerate for 2 hours.
2 To make the Cucumber Mint Yogurt, combine the yogurt, garlic, mint and cucumber. Mix until well combined. Cover and chill before serving.
3 Soak the bamboo skewers in water for 10 minutes, then drain. Thread the chicken pieces onto the bamboo skewers. Preheat a grill or stovetop grill pan, then brush the grill with the oil. Grill the chicken skewers until golden and tender, 2–3 minutes each side.
4 Steam or blanch the choy sum in boiling water for 3 minutes or until tender crisp, then drain. Serve the chicken warm with the Cucumber Mint Yogurt and steamed choy sum.

Serves 4

Garlic and Red Pepper Scallops

Five spice powder, soy sauce and rice wine—classic ingredients from China—are combined in this dish to create the perfect backdrop for sweet and succulent scallops. The rice wine complements the spicy chili pepper, creating a wonderful balance of flavors.

1 lb (500 g) shucked fresh scallops, cleaned
3 cloves garlic, finely chopped
1/2 teaspoon five spice powder
1 teaspoon peeled and grated fresh ginger
1 finger-length red chili pepper, deseeded and finely chopped
2 tablespoons soy sauce
1 tablespoon Chinese rice wine or dry sherry
2 tablespoons oil
3 tablespoons water
1 cup (30 g) watercress, young mustard greens or mizuna, for garnish

1 Place the scallops in a shallow nonmetallic dish. In a bowl, combine the garlic, five spice powder, ginger, chili pepper, soy sauce and rice wine, and pour over the scallops. Cover the dish with plastic wrap and refrigerate for 30 minutes. Drain the scallops, reserving the marinade. Preheat a grill or stovetop grill pan, then brush the grill with the oil. Grill the scallops until their translucent flesh turns white, 2–3 minutes, turning during cooking. Remove from the grill.

2 Place the reserved marinade into a saucepan. Add the water, bring to a boil and allow to boil for 1 minute; set aside. To serve, arrange the garnish on serving plates. Top with the scallops and drizzle with the warm marinade.

Serves 4

Two-Pepper Calamari

This simple dish allows the the wonderful, slightly sweet flavor of quick-cooking calamari to shine. The grilled calamari, which is the Italian word for squid, are served over a bed of pleasantly sharp greens—a refreshing counterpoint to the slightly spicy seasoning.

2 finger-length red chili peppers, deseeded
 and finely chopped
1 tablespoon salt
1 teaspoon cracked black pepper
16 baby squid (calamari), about 2 lb (1 kg),
 cleaned and halved
2 tablespoons oil
1 1/2 cups (45 g) watercress, young mustard
 greens or mizuna, for garnish

Combine the chili pepper, salt and pepper. Brush the squid pieces with oil and press the chili pepper mix into both sides of the squid. Preheat a grill or stovetop grill pan. Grill the squid pieces for 15–30 seconds on each side. Remove from the grill and serve on a bed of watercress.

Serves 2–4

Grilled Chicken with Asian Greens

The flavors of grilled garlicky chicken, easy-to-prepare rice noodles and crisp Asian salad greens make this delicious dish a perfect meal-in-one. The chicken can be served warm or chilled, if made the day ahead.

Handful dried rice vermicelli noodles

2 tablespoons oil

2 cloves garlic, finely chopped

2 small thin eggplants, thinly sliced lengthwise

2 whole boneless chicken breasts

2 cups (60 g) mixed Asian salad leaves (watercress, snow pea shoots, mizuna and tah soi)

1/4 cup (15 g) fresh bean sprouts, rinsed

8 cherry tomatoes, quartered

1/2 red onion, cut into very thin wedges

Sesame Ginger Dressing

2 teaspoons dark sesame oil

1 tablespoon oil

3 teaspoons peeled and grated fresh ginger

1/4 cup (60 ml) fresh lime juice

2 tablespoons mirin (sweet rice wine) or sweet sherry

1 Place the noodles into a heatproof bowl and cover with boiling water. Allow to stand until softened, about 10 minutes; drain. Using scissors, snip the noodles into shorter lengths.

2 Combine the oil and garlic in a bowl and brush the eggplant and chicken breasts with the mixture. Preheat a grill or stovetop grill pan and grill the eggplant slices until golden and tender, about 1 minute each side. Remove and cut each slice in half. Grill the chicken until golden and tender, about 4–5 minutes each side. Test the chicken by piercing the thickest part with a skewer; the chicken is cooked if the juices run clear. Remove from the grill and allow to stand 5 minutes before slicing each into 8 diagonal slices. Arrange the chicken on serving plates.

3 To make the Sesame Ginger Dressing, combine the oils, ginger, lime juice and mirin in a screw-top jar. Shake well to mix.

4 Combine the noodles, eggplant, salad leaves, bean sprouts, tomatoes and onion. Toss until well combined. Divide among serving plates. Drizzle with the Dressing and serve immediately.

Serves 4

Fresh Salmon Cakes

This twist on the classic salmon cake—combining flavors from the East and West—is a great way to enjoy this popular fish, which is high in protein and Omega-3 oils. For a quick shortcut, canned salmon can be used, but the cakes won't have the same intensity of grilled flavor.

1 lb (500 g) boneless and skinless fresh
  salmon fillets
2 tablespoons oil, divided in half
2 lbs (1 kg) baking potatoes, peeled and
  chopped
3 tablespoons chopped fresh dill
1–2 finger-length red chili peppers, deseeded and chopped
3 teaspoons peeled and grated fresh ginger
Grated zest of 1 lime
1 teaspoon salt
1/2 teaspoon freshly ground black pepper
2 eggs, beaten
2 tablespoons milk
1/2 cup (75 g) all-purpose flour
3 cups (180 g) fresh white breadcrumbs

1 Preheat a grill or stovetop grill pan, then brush the grill with 1 tablespoon of the oil. Grill the salmon until it flakes easily when tested with a fork, 3–4 minutes each side (salmon should be cooked completely through). Remove from the grill and allow to cool. Place the potatoes into a saucepan of boiling water and cook until tender, about 8 minutes, then drain and mash. Allow to cool for 10 minutes. Add the salmon, dill, chili peppers, ginger, zest, salt and pepper. Using wet hands, mix thoroughly. Cover with plastic wrap and refrigerate for 1 hour.

2 Divide into 12 portions and shape them into patties. Combine the egg and milk in a bowl. Dredge each patty in flour, dip into the egg-milk mixture, and then coat in breadcrumbs.

3 Preheat a grill or stovetop grill pan and carefully brush the grill with the remaining oil. Cook the salmon cakes until golden, 2–3 minutes each side. Remove from the grill and serve warm or chilled with Green Aioli (see page 55 for recipe).

Serves 4

Beef Satay Skewers

Satay, a Southeast Asian favorite, consists of skewered slices of seasoned meat or chicken grilled over a fire, then served with various sauces, depending on the particular satay traditions of each country or region. This satay marinade is a perfect blend of salty and sweet that will leave your guests asking for more.

12 bamboo skewers
1 lb (500 g) boneless sirloin steak
5 tablespoons soy sauce
2 tablespoons oyster sauce
1 teaspoon sugar
2 tablespoons mirin (rice wine) or sweet sherry
2 teaspoons dark sesame oil
1 clove garlic, minced
1 tablespoon chopped fresh coriander leaves (cilantro)
2 tablespoons oil

1 Soak the skewers in cold water for 10 minutes, then drain. Slice the steak into thin long strips, about 1 by 4 inches (2.5 by 10 cm). Thread the strips onto skewers and place in a shallow nonmetallic dish. In a bowl, combine 2 tablespoons of the soy sauce, the oyster sauce, sugar, mirin, sesame oil, garlic and coriander leaves, and mix well. Brush the marinade over the beef, cover with plastic wrap and refrigerate for 30 minutes. Drain off the marinade.
2 Preheat the grill or stovetop grill pan, then brush the grill surface with the oil. Grill the beef skewers until tender, 2–3 minutes. Remove from the grill and serve hot with the remaining soy sauce as a dipping sauce.

Serves 3–4

Chinese Barbecued Pork with Sweet Hoisin Sauce

This recipe celebrates the classic ingredients and flavors of Chinese barbecue—pork and hoisin, also known as Chinese barbecue sauce. Hoisin is a sweet soy-based sauce that gets a kick from garlic and chili peppers and a little tang from vinegar, giving a finger-licking goodness to all that it graces.

1 lb (500 g) pork tenderloin
3 tablespoons soy sauce
1 tablespoon hot bean paste
2 tablespoons hoisin sauce
4 cloves garlic, minced
$1/4$ teaspoon five spice powder
1 tablespoon shaved palm sugar or dark
  brown sugar
2 tablespoons oil
$1/4$ head Chinese (Napa) cabbage, sliced
  into thin shreds

Serves 4

1 Place the tenderloin in a shallow nonmetallic dish. In a bowl, combine the soy sauce, hot bean paste, hoisin sauce, garlic, five spice powder and sugar, and mix well. Pour the mixture over the tenderloin, cover the dish with plastic wrap and refrigerate for 2–3 hours. Drain the pork, reserving the marinade.
2 Preheat the grill or stovetop grill pan, then brush the grill surface with the oil. Grill the pork until tender, 4–5 minutes each side, brushing with the reserved marinade during cooking. Remove from the grill, wrap in aluminum foil and allow to stand for 5 minutes.
3 Cook the cabbage in a saucepan of boiling water until tender, 3–5 minutes. Drain the cabbage and spoon into serving bowls. Thickly slice the pork and serve on top of the warm cabbage.

Pork and Apple Skewers

Not surprisingly, the classic pairing of pork and apples is popular worldwide. Though apples are well-entrenched in Western cuisine, religion, and folklore, the ancestor of today's apple is thought to have originated in Asia—making this recipe a truly Asian flavor sensation.

24 bamboo skewers
1$^1/_4$ lbs (600 g) pork tenderloin, cut into
  1$^1/_2$-in (4-cm) cubes
2 red apples, cut into 12 wedges each
5 tablespoons oil
2 tablespoons fresh lime juice
1 tablespoon soy sauce
2 tablespoons chopped fresh coriander
  leaves (cilantro)
2 kaffir lime leaves, very finely sliced
1 tablespoon chopped fresh Thai basil
1 teaspoon salt
1 teaspoon freshly ground black pepper
1 clove garlic, finely chopped

1 Soak the skewers in cold water for 10 minutes, then drain. Place the pork and apple wedges onto skewers and place in a shallow nonmetallic dish. In a bowl, combine 3 tablespoons of the oil, the lime juice, soy sauce, coriander leaves, lime leaves, basil, salt, pepper and garlic and mix well. Brush over the pork and apple, cover the dish with plastic wrap and refrigerate for 30 minutes. Drain off the marinade.
2 Preheat a grill or stovetop grill pan, then brush the grill surface with the remaining oil. Grill the skewers until the pork is tender, 2–3 minutes per side. Remove from the grill and serve warm.

Serves 6–8

Spicy Grilled Chicken Kibbeh

Kibbeh, essentially a Middle Eastern meatball, is made with a variety of spice and herb combinations, but is always made with ground meat and bulghur wheat. This recipe can also be made with gound lamb—the most traditional kibbeh meat—or ground turkey.

24 small bamboo skewers
1/3 cup (90 g) fine bulghur (cracked wheat)
1 lb (500 g) boneless chicken breast or
  thigh, coarsely chopped
1/2 teaspoon ground allspice
1/4 teaspoon ground red pepper (cayenne)
1 teaspoon ground cumin
1/2 teaspoon salt
1/2 teaspoon freshly ground black pepper
1/2 onion, coarsely chopped
1/2 cup (20 g) well-packed fresh mint
  leaves, finely chopped
2 tablespoons oil
Lemon wedges, for serving

Citrus Dipping Sauce
2 tablespoons olive oil
1/4 cup (60 ml) fresh lemon juice
1/2 teaspoon cracked black pepper

Serves 6

1 To make the Citrus Dipping Sauce, combine the oil, lemon juice and pepper and chill before serving.

2 Soak the bamboo skewers in water for 10 minutes, then drain. Place the bulghur into a bowl and cover with cold water. Allow to stand 10 minutes then drain. Squeeze out excess liquid using your hands. Place the chicken, allspice, ground red pepper, cumin, salt, pepper and onion in a food processor and process until finely minced, about 30 seconds. Transfer the mixture to a bowl, add the bulghur and mint leaves, and mix until well combined. Divide into 24 portions. Shape each into a log shape and insert a skewer into each. Preheat a grill or stovetop grill pan, then lightly brush the grill with the oil. Grill the skewers until the kibbeh is golden and tender, about 3–4 minutes. Remove from the grill and serve warm with lemon wedges and the Dipping Sauce.

Marinated Tuna Steaks

Meaty tuna steaks are among the most satisfying of the ocean's catch. In this recipe tuna is cooked to medium-rare, which retains its succulent flavor and tender texture and contrasts with the crusty grilled exterior. If you prefer tuna medium or well-done, simply cook it longer.

4 fresh tuna steaks (about 8 oz/250 g each)
2 tablespoons soy sauce
1/3 cup (80 ml) mirin (rice wine) or sweet sherry
1 tablespoon dark sesame oil
1 teaspoon cracked black pepper
1 teaspoon ground cumin
1 teaspoon five spice powder
1 teaspoon sugar
1 teaspoon salt
1 1/2 cups (45 g) watercress, young mustard greens or mizuna, for serving
Lime wedges, for serving

Place the tuna into a shallow nonmetallic dish. In a bowl, combine the soy sauce, mirin and sesame oil and brush over the tuna. Cover the dish with plastic wrap and refrigerate for 30 minutes. Drain, reserving the marinade. Combine the pepper, cumin, five spice powder, sugar and salt and mix well. Rub the spice mix into both sides of the tuna steaks. Preheat a grill or stovetop grill pan. Grill the tuna, allowing it to remain pink in the center, 3–4 minutes each side. Remove from the grill and allow to stand for 3 minutes. Pour the reserved marinade into a small saucepan and bring to a boil over medium heat; boil for 1 minute, then set aside. Cut each tuna steak into wedges, arrange on serving plates and drizzle with the warm marinade. Serve with watercress and lime wedges.

Serves 4

Fish Steak with Sake Glaze

These grilled fish steaks are brightened with the zesty flavor of fresh lime zest and the astringency of sake (Japanese rice wne), and served warm on a bed of fresh spinach. Serve extra lime zest on the side to allow diners to add more zest to their taste.

4 fish steaks, about 7 oz (200 g) each
   (choose any fish with firm, white flesh,
   such as sea bass, grouper, halibut or cod)
2 teaspoons salt
1 teaspoon freshly ground black pepper
2 tablespoons oil
2 tablespoons sake
Juice and grated zest of 1 lime plus 2 tablespoons additional grated lime zest
2 cups (60 g) baby spinach leaves,
   for serving

Sprinkle both sides of the fish with salt and pepper. Preheat a grill or stovetop grill pan, then brush the grill surface with the oil. Grill the fish until it changes color and flakes easily with a fork, 2–3 minutes on each side. Remove from the grill and brush each steak with the combined sake, juice and zest. To serve, arrange the spinach leaves on serving plates and top with the fish steaks. Serve with extra lime zest.

Serves 4

Grilled Shrimp with Lime and Coriander

Both the lime and leaves of kaffir lime trees, native to Indonesia, are used to give a distinct flavor to dishes throughout Southeast Asia. The leaves, which impart an unmistakable and refreshing flora-citrus aroma to food, can be used fresh, frozen or dried.

$1^1/_2$ lbs (750 g) fresh jumbo shrimp (king prawns)
$1/_3$ cup (80 ml) oil
1 tablespoon dark sesame oil
1 tablespoon chopped fresh coriander leaves (cilantro)
3 kaffir lime leaves, finely shredded
3 cloves garlic, finely chopped
1 tablespoon Chinese rice wine or dry sherry
Lemon or lime wedges, for serving

Serves 4

1 Remove the heads from the shrimp. Pull out and remove the veins (a bamboo skewer is good for this), leaving the shell intact. Place the shrimp in a shallow nonmetallic dish. Combine the oils, coriander leaves, lime leaves, garlic and rice wine; mix well and pour over the shrimp. Cover with plastic wrap and refrigerate overnight.
2 Remove the shrimp from the marinade. Preheat a grill or stove-top grill pan. Grill the shrimp until they change color, 2–3 minutes each side. Remove from the grill and allow to cool 5 minutes before serving with fresh lemon or lime wedges.

Note: Place a bowl of cold water with a slice of lemon on the table and plenty of paper napkins alongside so guests can rinse their hands after peeling the shrimp.

Spicy Fish Nibbles with Coconut Sambal

Sambal, a multi-purpose condiment popular throughout Malaysia, Indonesia and southern India, is made in innumerable variations. The creamy cooling flavor of this coconut sambal is the perfect complement to mildly spicy fish bites.

1¼ lbs (600 g) firm white boneless, skinless fish fillets
1½ teaspoons ground turmeric
1 teaspoon salt
2 teaspoons cornstarch
¼ teaspoon ground red pepper (cayenne)
2 tablespoons oil
3 cups (450 g) steamed jasmine rice
2 tablespoons chopped fresh coriander leaves (cilantro)
Garlic chives, for garnish

Coconut Sambal
⅓ cup (45 g) unsweetened shredded (desiccated) coconut
3 tablespoons boiling water
½ teaspoon dried shrimp paste
1 kaffir lime leaf, very finely sliced
¼ onion, finely chopped
2 teaspoons fresh lemon juice

1 To make the Coconut Sambal, place the coconut in a heatproof bowl, pour in the boiling water and mix well. Add the shrimp paste, lime leaf, onion and lemon juice. Cover and refrigerate until ready to serve.

2 Cut the fish into ¾-inch by 2½-inch (2-cm by 6-cm) lengths. In a bowl, combine the turmeric, salt, cornstarch and chili powder, mix well and rub the spice mixture into the fish pieces. Preheat a grill or stovetop grill pan, then brush the grill surface with the oil. Grill the fish pieces until the fish is firm, 1–2 minutes each side. Remove from the grill. Combine the cooked rice with the coriander leaves. Serve the fish nibbles with rice and Coconut Sambal. Garnish with the garlic chives.

Serves 4

Mixed Seafood Skewers

Pastes are a great way to add flavor to grilled foods. They are related to spice rubs, but they do have some moisture—often oil—which binds the paste ingredients together and helps to keep food moist. The delicate flavors of fresh lemongrass in this paste goes great with fish and seafood.

12 bamboo skewers

$1/2$ lb (250 g) fresh jumbo shrimp (king prawns) peeled and deveined, leaving tails intact

$1/2$ lb (250 g) shucked fresh scallops, cleaned

$3/4$ lb (350 g) white fish fillets, cut into $1^1/2$-in (4-cm) cubes

4 tablespoons peanut oil, divided in half

$1/2$ onion, coarsely chopped

2 cloves garlic

2 teaspoons peeled and grated fresh ginger

2 stems lemongrass (inner part of thick white section only), chopped

1 teaspoon dried shrimp paste

4 tablespoons soy sauce

1 teaspoon chili oil

1 teaspoon dark sesame oil

1 cup (30 g) watercress, young mustard greens or mizuna, for serving

1 Soak the bamboo skewers in cold water for 10 minutes, drain. Pat the shrimp, scallops and fish dry with paper towels and thread alternately onto the skewers. Brush the seafood skewers with 2 tablespoons of the peanut oil, then place into a shallow non-metallic dish.

2 Place the onion, garlic, ginger, lemongrass, shrimp paste, the remaining oil, 1 tablespoon of the soy sauce, chili oil and sesame oil into a food processor and process until the mixture becomes a smooth paste, about 30 seconds. Brush the seafood with the spice paste, then cover the dish with plastic wrap and refrigerate for 30 minutes.

3 Preheat a grill or stovetop grill pan. Grill the skewers until the seafood changes color, 3–4 minutes each side. Remove from the grill. Serve warm with the watercress and remaining soy sauce as a dipping sauce.

Serves 4

Herb Crusted Salmon

Flavorful herbs and seasoning give salmon fillets a crusty, exterior that contrasts with the delicate, flakey interior, while just a pinch of chili flakes adds some excitement. Served with Garlic Mashed Potatoes, this hearty pairing will satisfy friends and family on a cool autumn or winter day.

4 tablespoons chopped fresh coriander
 leaves (cilantro)
1 tablespoon grated lime zest
2 teaspoons freshly ground black pepper
1 teaspoon salt
2 tablespoons chopped fresh chervil
Pinch of dried red chili flakes
1 clove garlic, finely chopped
4 tablespoons oil, divided in half
4 fresh salmon fillets (about 7 oz/200 g
 each), bones and skin removed

Garlic Mashed Potatoes
4 baking potatoes, peeled and chopped
1 tablespoon olive oil
3 cloves garlic, finely chopped
$1/2$ teaspoon salt

1 In a bowl, combine the coriander leaves, zest, pepper, salt, chervil, chili flakes and garlic and mix until well combined. Brush the salmon with 2 tablespoons of the oil, then lightly coat both sides of each salmon fillet with the herb mixture.
2 To make Garlic Mashed Potatoes, cook the potatoes in a saucepan of boiling salted water until tender, about 8 minutes. Drain and mash. Add the olive oil, garlic and salt, and mix until well combined.
3 Preheat a grill or stovetop grill pan, then brush the grill surface with the remaining oil. Grill the salmon 2–3 minutes each side (salmon should remain pink on the inside). Remove from the grill and allow to stand 3 minutes before slicing in half. Serve warm with the Garlic Mashed Potatoes.

Serves 4

Grilled Seafood with Thai Curry Sauce

Thai curry dishes, often identified solely by their color—yellow, red or green—are distinguished by the use of coconut cream or milk, which adds thickness and rich flavor. Green curry is the spiciest of the Thai curries, so start with small amounts of paste, increasing the amount according to your taste.

12 fresh jumbo shrimp (king prawns), peeled and deveined, leaving tails intact

1 lb (500 g) swordfish, cut into 2$^{1}/_{2}$-in (6-cm) chunks

16 fresh scallops, shucked and cleaned

$^{1}/_{4}$ cup (60 ml) plus 2 teaspoons peanut oil

$^{1}/_{2}$ lb (250 g) green beans

3–4 teaspoons ready-made Thai green curry paste or to taste

2 cloves garlic, finely chopped

1$^{1}/_{2}$ cups (375 ml) coconut milk

3 kaffir lime leaves, crushed

1 tablespoon fish sauce

2 teaspoons soy sauce

1 teaspoon shaved palm sugar or dark brown sugar

1 tablespoon chopped fresh basil leaves

1 tablespoon chopped fresh coriander leaves (cilantro)

Note: Curry pastes are made with red or green chili peppers and are readily available in bottles in the condiments section of most supermarkets or you can make your own. Store in the refrigerator after opening.

Serves 4

1 Pat the seafood dry with paper towels and brush with $^{1}/_{4}$ cup of the oil. Preheat a grill or stovetop grill pan. Working in batches, grill the shrimp until they change color, 2–3 minutes, then remove from the heat. Grill the scallops until their flesh turns opaque, 2–3 minutes, then remove from the heat. Grill the fish pieces until the flesh is firm, 2–3 minutes, then remove from the heat.

2 Blanch the green beans in a saucepan of boiling water for 2 minutes, then drain. Combine the beans and seafood, cover and keep warm.

3 Place the curry paste, 2 teaspoons of the oil and the garlic in a wok or saucepan. Cook while stirring over medium heat until aromatic, about 2 minutes. Stir in the coconut milk, lime leaves, fish sauce, soy sauce and sugar. Reduce the heat to low and simmer for 10 minutes. Do not allow to boil. Remove from the heat and stir in the basil and coriander leaves. Divide the seafood and beans among serving bowls and spoon the remaining curry sauce over each bowl. Serve with steamed jasmine rice.

Grilled Salmon with Lemon Wasabi Butter

Flavored butters add an elegant touch to any meal, and they allow each diner to easily adjust seasoning to their taste. For a time-saver, make extra flavored butter, wrap well and freeze for another meal.

$^1/_2$ cup (1 stick/125 g) butter, softened
2 teaspoons wasabi paste
Grated zest of 1 lime
1 tablespoon fresh lime juice
$^1/_2$ teaspoon freshly ground black pepper
4 fresh salmon fillets (about 7 oz/200 g each), skin and bones removed
2 tablespoons oil
Fresh coriander leaves (cilantro), for garnish

Crispy Fried Potatoes
3 baking potatoes, peeled and very thinly sliced
$^1/_2$ cup (125 ml) oil, for frying

Serves 4

1 Place the butter in a mixing bowl and beat until soft. Add the wasabi, zest, lime juice and pepper and mix until well combined. Refrigerate until firm.
2 Brush the salmon with the oil. Preheat a grill or stovetop grill pan. Grill the salmon 2–3 minutes on each side (salmon should remain pink in the center), then allow to stand for 5 minutes before cutting in half.
3 To make Crispy Fried Potatoes, pat the potatoes dry with paper towels. Heat the oil over medium heat and, working in batches, fry the potato slices until golden and crisp, about 2 minutes. Remove with a slotted spoon and drain on paper towels.
4 Place the grilled salmon fillets on serving plates. Using a teaspoon or melon baller, scoop the wasabi butter onto the fish. Serve with the Crispy Fried Potatoes and garnish with fresh coriander leaves.

Note: Leftover wasabi butter can be stored in a sealed container in the refrigerator for up to 2 weeks.

Grilled Tuna and Egg with Rosemary

This tuna and egg combination makes a unique brunch dish or an elegant lunch or dinner. A drizzle of slightly spicy Garlic Butter Sauce gives the simply prepared tuna and egg a burst of rich flavor and seasoning.

4 fresh tuna steaks (about 7 oz/200 g each)
8 small stems fresh rosemary
String
2 tablespoons oil
4 eggs

Garlic Butter Sauce
$^1/_4$ cup ($^1/_2$ stick/60 g) unsalted butter
3 cloves garlic, finely chopped
1 finger-length red chili pepper, deseeded
  and finely chopped
1 tablespoon chopped fresh coriander
  leaves (cilantro)
$^1/_4$ teaspoon salt
$^1/_4$ teaspoon freshly ground black pepper

1 Place the tuna steaks on a cutting board and top each steak with 2 stems of fresh rosemary. Secure the rosemary with string, tying it like a parcel. Preheat a grill or stovetop grill pan, then brush the grill with the oil. Grill the tuna 2 minutes on each side (the tuna should remain pink on the inside). Remove from the grill and keep warm.

2 To make the Garlic Butter Sauce, place the butter, garlic and red chili pepper in a small saucepan. Stir over medium heat until the butter melts. Cook until the butter bubbles, about 1 minute. Remove from the heat and stir in the coriander leaves, salt and pepper.

3 Poach the eggs in a saucepan of simmering salted water for 3–4 minutes. Remove with a slotted spoon and drain. To serve, place the tuna on serving plates, top each with a poached egg, then drizzle with the warm Garlic Butter Sauce.

Serves 4

Lime and Pepper Sardines with Green Aioli

Once thought too oily and strong in flavor for American taste, fresh sardines are increasingly becoming a favorite of restaurant chefs for their rich flavor. Packed in Omega-3 fatty acids, sardines are a healthy "brain food." Don't use canned sardines for this recipe; they are very different in flavor from the fresh fish.

36 fresh sardines, cleaned, heads removed and butterflied
4 tablespoons oil, divided in half
1 teaspoon grated lime zest
1 tablespoon fresh lime juice
1 finger-length red chili pepper, deseeded and finely chopped
1 tablespoon chopped fresh coriander leaves (cilantro)
1/4 teaspoon salt
1/4 teaspoon freshly ground black pepper
1 1/2 cups (45 g) watercress, young mustard greens or mizuna

Green Aioli
6 green onions (scallions), coarsely chopped
1/4 cup (10 g) chopped fresh basil leaves
3 cloves garlic, chopped
3 egg yolks
2 tablespoons fresh lemon juice
3/4 cup (180 ml) virgin olive oil
Dash of salt and freshly ground black pepper

1 Pat the sardines dry with paper towels and place in a shallow nonmetallic dish. Combine 2 tablespoons of the oil, zest, lime juice, chili pepper, coriander leaves, salt and pepper and mix well. Brush over the sardines and let stand for 5 minutes.
2 Preheat a grill or stovetop grill pan, then brush the grill surface with the remaining oil. Grill the sardines 1–2 minutes on each side. Remove from the grill and cover with aluminum foil to keep warm.
3 To make the Green Aioli, place the green onions, basil, garlic, egg yolks and lemon juice into a food processor. Process until smooth, about 30 seconds. Gradually add the olive oil while the food processor is running and process until the mixture becomes a thick sauce. Add the salt and pepper.
4 To serve, arrange the watercress on serving plates and top with the warm sardines. Serve with the Green Aioli.

Note: Leftover aioli can be stored in a screw-top jar in the refrigerator for a week.

Serves 6

Grilled Jumbo Shrimp Skewers

Easy-to-prepare skewered foods are always popular at barbecues. These festive skewers contain a variety of bite-size food in different textures, flavors and colors, making them as enticing as they are delicious.

12 bamboo skewers
12 fresh jumbo shrimp (king prawns)
  peeled, deveined, leaving tails intact
4 tablespoons oil, divided in half
3 tablespoons fresh lime juice
2 teaspoons peeled and grated fresh ginger
2 cloves garlic, finely chopped
2 limes, cut into 6 wedges each
12 finger-length red chili peppers
2 red onions, cut into 6 wedges each
1^1/$_2$ cups (45 g) mixed salad greens, for
  serving

Serves 3–4

1 Soak the bamboo skewers in cold water for 10 minutes, then drain. Place the shrimp in a shallow nonmetallic dish. Combine 2 tablespoons of the oil, lime juice, ginger and garlic, mix well and pour over the shrimp. Cover the dish with plastic wrap, and refrigerate for 1 hour. Remove the shrimp from the marinade.
2 Thread a shrimp, lime wedge, chili pepper and red onion wedge onto each skewer. Preheat a grill or stovetop grill pan, then brush the grill surface with the remaining oil. Grill the skewers until the shrimp change color, 2–3 minutes each side. Remove from the grill and serve warm with the salad greens.

Grilled Sesame Tuna

Tiny sesame seeds—a favorite flavoring component in Asian cuisine—pack a lot of flavor and provide a nice encrusted exterior for many types of grilled fish. Fast-cooking rice noodles are the perfect accompaniament to this classic combination of tuna and sesame.

1 egg white
1 tablespoon soy sauce
4 fresh tuna steaks, about 7 oz (200 g) each
$1/_3$ cup (30 g) sesame seeds
2 tablespoons oil
4 oz (125 g) dried rice vermicelli noodles
1 tablespoon dark sesame oil
Lemon wedges, for serving

Serves 4

1 In a bowl, lightly beat the egg white with a fork and add the soy sauce. Brush one side of each tuna steak with the egg white mixture, then dip the egg white side of the tuna into the sesame seeds. Preheat a grill or stovetop grill pan, then brush the grill surface with the oil. Grill the tuna, sesame seed side down first, for 2–3 minutes on each side (tuna should remain pink on the inside). Remove from the grill and allow to stand for 5 minutes before slicing in half. Cover with aluminum foil to keep warm.
2 To make the rice stick noodles, place the noodles in a heatproof bowl and cover with boiling water. Allow to soften for 15 minutes, then drain. Or cook in a saucepan of boiling water for 3 minutes, then drain.
3 Warm the sesame oil in a small saucepan over medium heat for 1 minute. To serve, place the tuna on a serving plate and drizzle with the warm sesame oil. Serve with the wam rice noodles and a wedge of fresh lemon.

Grilled Chicken Breast with Eggplant

A complex marinade—accented with mirin, fish sauce, soy sauce and fresh herbs—adds mouth-watering flavor to tender grilled chicken breast and serves as the basis for a delicious sauce to top over all. Tart eggplant and pleasantly sharp greens provide a satisfying accompaniment to the flavorful chicken.

4 boneless, skinless chicken breast halves

4 green onions (scallions), coarsely chopped

4 cloves garlic

1 tablespoon chopped fresh basil leaves

1 tablespoon chopped fresh coriander leaves (cilantro)

1/3 cup (80 ml) soy sauce

1 teaspoon five spice powder

2 tablespoons mirin (rice wine) or sweet sherry

1 tablespoon fish sauce

1 teaspoon dark sesame oil

2 teaspoons sugar

Oil

6 small thin eggplants, sliced lengthwise into 1/16-in (2-mm) slices

2 cups (60 g) watercress, young mustard greens or mizuna leaves, for serving

Serves 4

1 Place the chicken in a shallow nonmetallic dish. Place the green onions, garlic, basil, coriander leaves, soy sauce, five spice powder, mirin, fish sauce, sesame oil and sugar in a food processor and process until well blended, about 30 seconds. Pour the marinade over the chicken, cover the dish with plastic wrap and refrigerate for 2 hours. Drain the chicken, reserving the marinade.

2 Preheat a grill or stovetop grill pan, then brush the grill surface lightly with oil. Grill the chicken breasts until golden and tender, 4–5 minutes each side, brushing with the reserved marinade during cooking. Test the chicken by piercing the thickest part with a skewer; the chicken is cooked if the juices run clear. Remove from the grill. Lightly brush the eggplant slices with oil and grill until golden and tender, 1–2 minutes each side. Place the reserved marinade in a small saucepan and stir over medium heat and bring to a boil; allow to boil for 1 minute, then set aside.

3 To serve, arrange the watercress on serving plates, top with some eggplant slices and then a chicken breast. Drizzle with the warm marinade.

Five Spice Grilled Chicken

Some theorize that Chinese five spice powder symbolizes the five elements. This near mystical spice blend—which consists of equal parts ground cinnamon, cloves, star anise, fennel seeds and Szechuan peppercorns—adds a rich complexity to grilled chicken that will leave your guests asking for seconds.

2 lbs (1 kg) bone-in chicken pieces
1 teaspoon dark sesame oil
1 tablespoon mirin (rice wine) or sweet
  sherry
4 tablespoons peanut oil, divided in half
1 teaspoon five spice powder
1 teaspoon peeled and grated fresh ginger
1 clove garlic, minced
1 tablespoon honey
2 tablespoons soy sauce
1 red onion, cut into 8 wedges
1 bunch (about 1 lb/500 g) choy sum,
  broccoli rabe, or mustard greens

Serves 4

1 Rinse the chicken pieces in running water, pat dry with paper towels and place them in a shallow nonmetallic dish.
2 In a small bowl, combine the sesame oil, mirin, 2 tablespoons of the peanut oil, the five spice powder, ginger, garlic, honey and soy sauce, and mix well. Brush the mixture over the chicken skin, then cover the dish with plastic wrap and refrigerate for 3 hours. Drain the chicken, reserving the marinade.
3 Preheat the grill, then lightly brush the cooking grate with the remaining peanut oil. Grill the chicken pieces until golden and tender, about 8 minutes on each side, brushing with the reserved marinade during cooking. Test the chicken by piercing the thickest part with a skewer; chicken is cooked if the juices run clear. Remove from the grill.
4 Grill the onion wedges until lightly browned, 1–2 minutes. Steam or blanch the choy sum in boiling water until tender-crisp, about 2 minutes; drain. To serve, place the choy sum on 4 serving plates, top with the chicken, and garnish with red onion wedges.

Note: This recipe is best suited to an outdoor grill. However, if only an indoor grill pan is available, grill the chicken until golden, then bake in a 350°F (180°C) oven for 10–15 minutes to cook through. Otherwise substitute quicker-cooking boneless chicken breasts for bone-in chicken pieces.

Grilled Thai Coconut Chicken

Coconut milk, a staple in Thai cuisine, adds a velvety richness to this chicken dish and is also an indispensable counterpoint to the fiery hot chili peppers.

1¼ cups (300 ml) coconut milk
3 cloves garlic, minced
2 finger-length red chili peppers, deseeded and minced
1 teaspoon peeled and grated fresh ginger
½ cup (30 g) fresh coriander leaves (cilantro)
Grated zest and juice of 1 lime
3 tablespoons soy sauce
1 tablespoon fish sauce
1 tablespoon grated palm sugar or dark brown sugar
4 boneless chicken breast halves
1 tablespoon oil
1 bunch (¾ lb/400 g) bok choy, rinsed and cut in half lengthwise

Serves 4

1 To make the marinade, place the coconut milk, garlic, chili peppers, ginger, coriander leaves, lime zest, juice, soy sauce, fish sauce and sugar in a food processor or blender. Process until smooth, about 30 seconds.

2 Place the chicken breasts on a cutting board and make 3 slits in the skin side of each using a sharp knife. Place the chicken in a shallow nonmetallic dish. Pour the marinade ingredients over the chicken and cover the dish with plastic wrap. Refrigerate for 2 hours. Drain the chicken, reserving the marinade.

3 Preheat the grill or stovetop grill pan, then lightly brush the grill surface with the oil. Grill the chicken until tender, 4–5 minutes on each side. Test the chicken by piercing the thickest part with a skewer; the chicken is cooked if the juices run clear. Remove from the grill.

4 Steam or blanch the bok choy in a saucepan of boiling water until tender crisp, about 2 minutes. Place the reserved marinade in a small saucepan. Bring to a boil over medium heat, stirring frequently. Boil for one minute, remove from the heat and set aside.

5 To serve, arrange the bok choy on 4 serving plates and top each with a chicken piece. Drizzle with the warm marinade. Serve any extra marinade in a separate serving bowl.

Grilled Marinated Chicken with Ginger Risotto

Star anise gets its name from its striking star-shaped appearance. Here the slightly bitter flavor of this dried pod is balanced with a touch of honey and rice wine to create a subtle and exotic marinade. Native to China, star anise is one of the key ingredients in five spice powder, a classic Chinese spice blend.

4 boneless chicken breast halves

4 tablespoons oil, divided in half

1 tablespoon Chinese rice wine or dry
  sherry

1 tablespoon soy sauce

1 tablespoon honey

2 tablespoons peeled and grated fresh
  ginger

2 cloves garlic, finely chopped

2 whole star anise pods

Ginger Risotto

5 1/2 cups (1.25 liters) chicken stock

2 whole star anise pods

3 tablespoons olive oil

1 onion, chopped

1 clove garlic, finely chopped

2 teaspoons peeled and grated fresh ginger

1 1/2 cups (330 g) arborio (risotto) rice

1/4 cup (10 g) chopped fresh coriander
  leaves (cilantro)

Salt and freshly ground black pepper to
  taste

Serves 4

1 Using a sharp knife, pierce the skin side of each chicken breast 3–5 times. Place the chicken in a shallow nonmetallic dish. In a bowl, combine 2 tablespoons of the oil, rice wine, soy sauce, honey, ginger, garlic and star anise and pour over the chicken. Cover the dish with plastic wrap and refrigerate for 3 hours. Drain the chicken, reserving the marinade.

2 To make the Ginger Risotto, place the stock and star anise into a medium-sized saucepan and bring to a boil over high heat. Reduce the heat to low and allow the stock to simmer. Warm the oil in a medium-large saucepan over medium heat. Add the onion, garlic and ginger and cook, stirring, until the onion softens, about 2 minutes. Add the rice, cook for 1 minute, stirring constantly until the rice is coated with oil. Add 1 cup of the stock to the pan, stirring constantly. Reduce the heat, and allow to simmer gently while stirring. Gradually add the remaining stock 1 cup at a time until the rice is tender yet firm and creamy. This will take about 20–25 minutes. Stir in the coriander leaves and season with salt and pepper. Cover to keep warm until serving.

3 Preheat a grill or stovetop grill pan, then brush the grill surface with the remaining oil. Grill the chicken until golden and tender, 4–5 minutes each side, brushing with the reserved marinade during cooking. Test the chicken by piercing the thickest part with a skewer; the chicken is cooked if the juices run clear. Remove from the grill.

4 To serve, spoon the warm Ginger Risotto on serving plates and top with the chicken.

Barbecued Chicken or Cornish Hens

This elegant twist on the ubiquitous barbecued chicken uses small, individual-sized Cornish hens. Marinated in a delicous peppery-sweet sauce, these easy-to prepare hens will soon become a favorite meal for special weekday dinners or when entertaining. Alternatively, half-chickens will also barbecue beautifully.

2 small chickens, 3–4 lbs (1.5 kg) each, cut in half, or 4 Cornish hens, 1 lb (500 g) each
$1/3$ cup (80 ml) soy sauce
1 teaspoon sugar
3 tablespoons mirin (rice wine) or sweet sherry
1 tablespoon peeled and grated fresh ginger
4 tablespoons olive oil, divided in half
2 cups (60 g) salad greens such as watercress and snowpea shoots, for serving

Serves 4

1 Clean the chicken halves or hens and pat them dry with paper towels. Place the chicken halves (or hens) in a nonmetallic dish. If you're barbecuing hens, truss the wings and legs securely with wetted string. Combine the soy sauce, sugar, mirin, ginger and 2 tablespoons of the olive oil, and brush over the chicken or hens. Cover the dish with plastic wrap and refrigerate for 1 hour. Drain, reserving the marinade.

2 Preheat a grill, then brush the cooking grate with the remaining oil. Grill the chicken halves or hens until golden and tender, about 12–15 minutes for the chicken and 25–35 minutes for the hens, brushing with the reserved marinade and turning them during cooking. Test for doneness by piercing the thickest part of the chicken or hen with a skewer; the meat is cooked if the juices run clear. Remove from the heat and serve hot or cold with salad greens.

Note: This recipe can also be used with chicken pieces.

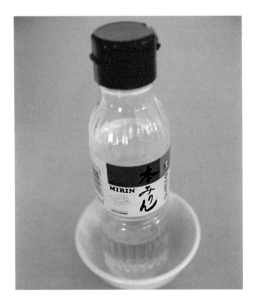

Grilled Chicken and Pesto Pizzettas

In this recipe fresh coriander leaves and chili oil provide a subtle Asian twist on the classic pesto pizza. These miniature pizzas are great taste treats to serve at parties.

Coriander Basil Pesto

3/4 cup (30 g) well-packed fresh basil leaves

1/4 cup (10 g) well-packed fresh coriander leaves (cilantro)

3 cloves garlic

1/2 cup (60 g) pine nuts

1/2 cup (60 g) freshly grated parmesan cheese

1/3 cup (80 ml) virgin olive oil

Grilled Chili Chicken

2 boneless chicken breast halves

4 cloves garlic, finely chopped

2 finger-length red chili peppers, deseeded and finely chopped

4 tablespoons oil, divided in half

Pizzettas

4 tablespoons tomato paste

2 cloves garlic, finely chopped

2 teaspoons chili oil

2 ready-made pizza bases, 12-in (30-cm) each

24 baby arugula leaves or baby spinach, rinsed, for garnish

Makes 12 pizzettas

1 To make Coriander Basil Pesto, place the basil and coriander leaves in a food processor and process until finely chopped, about 30 seconds. Add the garlic, pine nuts and cheese and process until finely ground, about 30 seconds. With the food processor running, gradually add the olive oil and process until the mixture becomes a thick paste, about 1 minute.

2 To make Grilled Chili Chicken, using a sharp knife, pierce the skin side of each chicken breast 3–5 times, and place the chicken in a shallow nonmetallic dish. In a bowl, combine the garlic, chili peppers and 2 tablespoons of the oil and pour over the chicken. Cover the dish with plastic wrap and refrigerate for 1 hour; drain.

3 Preheat a grill or stovetop grill pan, then brush the cooking grate with the remaining oil. Grill the chicken until golden and tender, 4–5 minutes each side. Test the chicken by piercing the thickest part with a skewer; the chicken is cooked if the juices run clear. Remove from the grill and allow to stand 5 minutes before thinly slicing diagonally.

4 To assemble the Pizzettas, preheat the oven to 350°F (180°C). In a bowl, combine the tomato paste, garlic and chili oil; mix well. Remove the pizza bases from packaging and cut into 4-inch (10-cm) rounds using a cookie (biscuit) cutter and spread each with a little tomato paste mix. Place on a baking tray lined with parchment (baking paper). Bake at 350°F (180°C) until crisp, 12–15 minutes. Remove from the oven and top each with a spoonful of pesto, a couple of arugula leaves and slices of grilled chicken. Serve warm as a snack or with drinks when entertaining.

Note: Leftover pesto, topped with a thin covering of oil, can be stored in a screw-top jar in the refrigerator for 3–4 days.

Fragrant Chicken and Pork Patties with Asian Herbs

Hamburgers are a dime a dozen at barbecues. Why not surprise your friends and family with these chicken-and-pork patties that are bursting with unexpected flavor? The richer and fattier pork helps chicken hold up to the high heat of the grill, creating mouthwatering patties.

1 lb (500 g) ground chicken, preferably thigh meat

1/2 lb (250 g) ground lean pork

8 green onions (scallions), chopped

3 cloves garlic, finely chopped

3 finger-length red chili peppers, 1 deseeded and finely chopped, 2 deseeded and sliced

1/4 cup (10 g) finely chopped fresh coriander leaves (cilantro)

2 teaspoons grated lime zest

2 tablespoons fresh lime juice

1 1/2 cups (90 g) fresh white breadcrumbs

1 egg, beaten

2 tablespoons oil, divided in half

12 fresh basil leaves

1 head baby Romaine lettuce, leaves separated and washed, for garnish

1 Place the chicken, pork, green onions, garlic, chopped chili pepper, coriander leaves, zest, lime juice, breadcrumbs and egg in a large mixing bowl. Using wet hands, mix until well combined. Divide into 12 portions and shape each into a round patty. Place in a single layer on a plate, cover with plastic wrap and refrigerate for 1 hour.

2 Preheat a grill or stovetop grill pan, then brush the grill surface with 1 tablespoon of the oil. Grill the patties until golden and tender, 2–3 minutes each side. Remove from the grill. Heat the remaining oil in a small saucepan over medium heat and fry the basil leaves and the 2 sliced chili peppers until aromatic, about 1 minute.

3 To serve, place the chicken patties on serving plates with lettuce leaves and top each with the fried basil and chili peppers.

Serves 4

Grilled Steak with Zesty Coriander Basil Butter

Nothing satisfies like a grilled steak, and nothing could be easier or quicker to prepare. A good-quality steak requires nothing more than salt and pepper. Yet, with the simple addition of a flavored butter, a simple steak is transformed into an elegant meal—perfect for entertaining or when you feel like treating yourself.

$1/_2$ cup (1 stick/125 g) butter, softened
2 tablespoons chopped fresh coriander
  leaves (cilantro)
2 tablespoons chopped fresh basil leaves
2 teaspoons grated lime zest
$1/_2$ finger-length red chili pepper, deseeded
  and chopped (optional)
$1/_2$ teaspoon freshly ground black pepper
$6^1/_2$ oz (200 g) dried buckwheat noodles or
  whole wheat pasta
4 rib eye steaks, about 8 oz (250 g) each
1 tablespoon olive oil
5 teaspoons chili oil

1 Place the butter into a mixing bowl and beat until soft. Add the coriander leaves, basil, zest, chili pepper and black pepper and mix until well combined. Spoon onto a piece of plastic wrap, roll into a log shape and refrigerate until firm, about 15 minutes.
2 Cook the buckwheat noodles or pasta in a saucepan of boiling water until tender, 5–6 minutes; drain.
3 Brush the steaks with the combined olive oil and 1 teaspoon of the chili oil. Preheat a grill or stovetop grill pan. Grill the steaks until cooked to your liking (for medium-rare, cook about 3–4 minutes per side). Remove from the grill and place on serving plates.
4 Slice the butter into $1/_4$-inch (6-mm) rounds and place on the hot steaks. Serve with buckwheat noodles and the remaining chili oil for dipping.

Serves 4

Beef Tenderloin with Papaya Relish

This beef tenderloin—infused with the subtle taste of fresh coriander leaves, basil and chili oil, and served with prosciutto and fruit salsa—is a sensational combination of salty, sweet and savory. For more dramatic presentation when entertaining, carve the tenderloin tableside.

1$^1/_2$ lbs (750 g) beef tenderloin
2 teaspoons chili oil
3 tablespoons chopped fresh basil leaves
2 tablespoons chopped fresh coriander
 leaves (cilantro)
4 tablespoons oil, divided in half
6 thin slices prosciutto (Italian ham)

Papaya Relish
$^1/_2$ small fresh papaya, peeled,
 deseeded and chopped
4 shallots, sliced
$^1/_3$ cup (80 ml) bottled Thai sweet chili
 sauce
2 tablespoons chopped fresh basil leaves
2 tablespoons chopped fresh coriander
 leaves (cilantro)

Serves 4–6

1 To make the Papaya Relish, combine the papaya, shallots, Thai sweet chili sauce (see page 15), basil and coriander leaves, and mix well. Refrigerate until serving.
2 Truss the beef with string to hold in shape and place in a shallow nonmetallic dish. In a bowl, combine the chili oil, basil, coriander leaves and 2 tablespoons of the oil and mix well. Spread the mixture over the meat, cover the dish with plastic wrap and refrigerate for 1 hour.
3 Meanwhile, grill or pan-fry the prosciutto until golden and crisp. Remove and drain on paper towels. Allow to cool, then break each in half and set aside.
4 Preheat a grill, then brush the cooking grate with the remaining oil. Grill the beef for 12–15 minutes, turning during cooking. Remove from the grill, wrap in aluminum foil and allow to stand for 10 minutes, then cut into 4 thick steaks. To serve, place the crisp prosciutto pieces on serving plates, top with a steak and spoon the Papaya Relish over top. Serve immediately.

Grilled Beef with Fresh Chili Salsa

Much of what makes Asian barbecue so delicious are the numerous dipping sauces, chutneys, relishes and other condiments that provide flavor, spice and contrast. This delicious salsa is best prepared in the summer when garden-ripe tomatoes are readily available.

2 lbs (1 kg) sirloin or porterhouse steak
1 teaspoon dark sesame oil
3 tablespoons oil
3 cloves garlic, chopped
$1/4$ cup (10 g) fresh coriander leaves
   (cilantro)
$1/4$ cup (10 g) chopped fresh basil leaves
1 cup (30 g) fresh watercress, for garnish

Fresh Chili Salsa
1 small ripe tomato, finely chopped
1 finger-length red chili pepper, deseeded
   and finely chopped
$1/4$ red onion, finely chopped
2 kaffir limes leaves, finely shredded
3 tablespoons fish sauce
2 tablespoons fresh lime juice
2 teaspoons shaved palm sugar or dark
   brown sugar

1 To make the Fresh Chili Salsa, combine the tomato, chili pepper, onion, lime leaves, fish sauce, juice and sugar and mix well. Cover and refrigerate until serving.
2 Remove any excess fat from the meat and place in a shallow nonmetallic dish. Place the sesame oil, 1 tablespoon of the oil, garlic, coriander leaves and basil in a food processor and process until the mixture becomes a thick paste, about 30 seconds. Spread the paste over both sides of the meat. Cover the dish with plastic wrap and refrigerate for 1 hour.
3 Preheat a grill or stovetop grill pan, then brush the grill surface with the remaining oil. Grill the steak, 3–4 minutes per side (for medium-rare doneness). Remove from the grill, cover with aluminum foil and allow to stand for 5 minutes. Using a sharp knife, slice the steak thinly and serve with the Fresh Chili Salsa, garnished with fresh watercress.

Serves 4

Barbecued Rack of Lamb with Asian Spices

Lamb is known for its tender meat and uniquely delicious flavor. Here lamb is marinated for 3–4 hours in a classic Asian herb and spice blend of fresh coriander leaves, cumin and ground coriander. The extra long marinade creates an aromatic and irresistible rack of lamb.

$1/_3$ cup (80 ml) fresh lime juice
$1/_3$ cup (80 ml) plus 2 tablespoons olive oil
3 tablespoons chopped fresh coriander leaves (cilantro)
5 cloves garlic, finely chopped
2 teaspoons salt
1 teaspoon freshly ground black pepper
1 tablespoon ground cumin
1 teaspoon ground coriander
2 racks of lamb, 8 cutlets each, excess fat trimmed
4 limes, cut in half
Bottled Thai Sweet Chili Sauce, for serving

1 In a bowl, combine the lime juice, $1/_3$ cup of the olive oil, coriander leaves, garlic, salt, pepper, cumin and ground coriander and mix until well combined. Place the lamb in a shallow non-metallic dish and brush with the herb mixture. Cover the dish with plastic wrap and refrigerate for 3–4 hours. Remove the lamb from the marinade.

2 Preheat a grill or stovetop grill pan, then brush the grill surface with 2 tablespoons of the oil. Grill the lamb until just pink in the center when cut, about 8 minutes each side. Remove from the heat, cover with aluminum foil and allow to stand for 5 minutes. Barbecue the lime halves until lightly golden, 1–2 minutes. Slice the lamb racks into 2 cutlet sections and serve warm with the limes and Thai Sweet Chili Sauce (see page 15).

Serves 6–8

Korean Barbecued Steak

Korean barbecue is famous worldwide. With this quick-and-easy recipe, you can enjoy its signature flavors with little preparation. Grilled Asian pear is a delicious combination with the savory but slightly sweet steak.

2 lbs (1 kg) rib eye steak
3 tablespoons soy sauce
1 tablespoon sugar
3 cloves garlic, finely chopped
2 teaspoons peeled and grated fresh ginger
1 tablespoon dark sesame oil
3 tablespoons oil
2 tablespoons toasted sesame seeds
1 Asian (nashi) pear, cut into very thin slices
2 green onions (scallions), for garnish
$1/2$ head iceberg lettuce, cut into 4 wedges

Serves 4

1 Place the steak in a freezer bag and freeze for 1 hour. Remove from the freezer, slice very thinly and place in a nonmetallic dish. In a bowl, combine the soy sauce, sugar, garlic, ginger, sesame oil, 1 tablespoon of the oil and 1 tablespoon of the sesame seeds, and mix well. Pour over the sliced meat and mix until well combined. Cover the dish with plastic wrap and refrigerate for 30 minutes. Drain off the marinade.
2 Preheat a grill or stovetop grill pan, then brush the grill surface with the remaining oil. Grill the meat for 30 seconds each side. Remove from the grill. Grill the pear wedges until lightly golden, about 30 seconds. Cut the green onions into thin $2^1/_2$-inch (6-cm) long strips and place into a bowl of iced water until they curl, about 5 minutes; drain. Serve the sliced beef with grilled pear and a wedge of lettuce. Garnish with the green onion curls and remaining sesame seeds.

Sweet and New Potato Skewers

These grilled potato skewers are great year-round, but seem especially welcome on a crisp autumn day when root vegetables are in abundance. They make a wonderful main course for vegetarians or a perfect side dish for meat lovers.

12 long woody stems of fresh rosemary
1¹/₂ lbs (750 g) sweet potatoes
12 small new potatoes
2 tablespoons oil
1 teaspoon chili oil
1 teaspoon dried thyme leaves
2 cloves garlic, finely chopped
1 teaspoon salt
¹/₄ teaspoon freshly ground black pepper
¹/₃ cup (80 ml) bottled Thai sweet chili
  sauce, for dipping

Serves 3–4

1 Trim the rosemary stems to 6 inches (15 cm) long and remove the leaves 4 inches (10 cm) from base of stem. Soak the stems in cold water for 30 minutes, then drain.

2 Peel the sweet potatoes and cut into 1¹/₂-inch (4-cm) cubes. Cook the sweet potato cubes and new potatoes in a large saucepan of salted water until tender when pierced with a skewer, 8–10 minutes. Drain and refresh under cold running water. Pat the vegetables dry with paper towels and cut each new potato in half.

3 Thread the potatoes carefully onto the rosemary stems and place in a shallow dish. In a bowl, combine the oils, thyme leaves, garlic, salt and pepper and brush over the potatoes. Cover the dish with plastic wrap and stand for 30 minutes. Preheat a grill or stovetop grill pan, then grill the potato and rosemary skewers until golden, 1–2 minutes each side. Remove from the grill and serve hot with Thai sweet chili sauce (see page 15) as a dipping sauce.

Grilled Tofu Skewers with Satay Sauce

For centuries a prime source of protein in Asia, tofu has been steadily growing in popularity in the West over the last few decades. Economical and versatile tofu readily takes on the flavor of marinades and seasonings and is a great food to add to your grilling repertoire.

12 bamboo skewers
12 oz (375 g) firm pressed tofu, cut into
  $1^1/_4$-in (3-cm) cubes
8 green onions (scallions) cut into
  2-in (5-cm) lengths
2 tablespoons soy sauce
1 teaspoon dark sesame oil
1 clove garlic, finely chopped
2 tablespoons oil

Satay Sauce
3 tablespoons unsweetened chunky peanut
  butter
4 cloves garlic, chopped
1 teaspoon chili oil
2 tablespoons soy sauce
Pinch of salt
2 teaspoons sugar
2 tablespoons hot water
1 tablespoon hot bean paste

1 To make the Satay Sauce, place the peanut butter, garlic, chili oil, soy sauce, salt, sugar, hot water and hot bean paste into a food processor. Process until smooth.
2 Soak the skewers in cold water for 10 minutes, then drain. Place the tofu and green onion lengths alternately onto bamboo skewers and place in a shallow dish. In a bowl, combine the soy sauce, sesame oil and garlic and brush over the tofu and green onions. Cover the dish with plastic wrap and refrigerate for 30 minutes. Drain off the marinade.
3 Preheat a grill or stovetop grill pan, then cook the tofu and green onion skewers until golden, 1–2 minutes each side. Remove from the grill and serve warm with the Satay Sauce.

Note: Leftover satay sauce can be stored in a screw-top jar in the refrigerator for up to 7 days.

Serves 3–4

Grilled Polenta with Stir-fried Shrimp

This recipe takes a few more steps than most in this book but is well worth the extra effort. Polenta is a mush made from cornmeal, which in itself doesn't sound particularly appealing. Yet, when enhanced with butter, cheese and seasonings, formed into cakes and grilled, it is transformed into savory goodness.

Grilled Polenta Cakes

$1^1/_2$ cups (250 g) uncooked polenta (cornmeal)

$1/_3$ cup (15–20 g) finely chopped fresh basil leaves

3 cloves garlic, finely chopped

$1/_4$ cup (30 g) freshly grated Parmesan cheese

$1/_4$ cup ($1/_2$ stick/60 g) butter

2 tablespoons olive oil

Stir-fried Shrimp

2 tablespoons oil

3 cloves garlic, crushed

1 finger-length red chili pepper, deseeded and chopped

2 lbs (1 kg) fresh jumbo shrimp (king prawns) peeled and deveined, leaving tails intact

4 vine ripened tomatoes, stems removed and chopped

1 cup (30 g) loosely packed fresh basil leaves

1 To make the Grilled Polenta Cakes, cook the polenta as directed on package. Remove from the heat and stir in the basil, garlic, cheese and butter, mixing until the butter melts. Spoon the polenta into an oiled 8-inch by 10-inch (20-cm by 25-cm) shallow pan and smooth the surface with a spatula. Set aside and allow to cool for 1 hour. Turn out the polenta onto a cutting board and cut into 6 rectangles. Brush both sides of the polenta pieces with olive oil. Preheat a grill or stovetop grill pan and grill the polenta cakes until golden, 2–3 minutes each side. Remove from the grill. Serve warm with the stir-fried shrimp.

2 To make the Stir-fried Shrimp, warm the oil in a wok or skillet. Add the garlic and chili pepper and stir-fry over medium heat until aromatic, about 1 minute. Add the shrimp and stir-fry until they change color, 4–5 minutes. Add the tomato and stir-fry for 2 minutes. Remove from the heat, add the basil leaves and toss through. Serve immediately.

Serves 6

Grilled Vegetables with Warm Ginger Dressing

These vegetables are full of flavors and textures that will delight your taste buds—the sweet anise flavor of fennel, tart flavor of eggplants, tender springtime essence of asparagas and crunchy texture of quick-cooking bok choy. The bright acidity and peppery notes of the Warm Ginger Dressing adds an elegant touch.

2 tablespoons oil
3 cloves garlic, finely chopped
2 baby fennel, cut in half lengthwise
4 baby bok choy, cut in half lengthwise
4 small eggplants (aubergines), cut in
  half lengthwise
2 red onions, cut into 6 wedges each
2 red chili peppers, cut in half lengthwise
12 fresh asparagus spears, trimmed

Warm Ginger Dressing
1 tablespoon dark sesame oil
2 tablespoons oil
1 tablespoon peeled and grated fresh ginger
$1/3$ cup (80 ml) fresh lime juice
2 tablespoons mirin (rice wine) or sweet
  sherry

1 To make the Warm Ginger Dressing, place the oils, ginger, lime juice and mirin in a small saucepan. Whisk over a low heat until just warm, about 1 minute. Rewarm over low heat for about 30 seconds just before serving.
2 In a large bowl, combine the oil and garlic and then add the vegetables. Toss through until the vegetables are well coated.
3 Preheat a grill or stovetop grill pan. Working in batches, grill the vegetables until golden, 1–2 minutes each side. Remove from the grill, place into serving bowls and drizzle with the Warm Ginger Dressing. Serve immediately.

Serves 2–4

Honey Glazed Pears with Sweet Rice Pudding

Surprise your guests with this sweet ending from the grill. Any firm pear can be grilled, but make sure it is ripe for optimum flavor.

Sweet Rice Pudding
1 cup (220 g) uncooked short grain rice
5 cups (1.25 liters) milk
1 vanilla bean
$^1/_2$ cup (100 g) superfine (caster) sugar
$^3/_4$ cup (185 ml) light cream

Grilled Honey Glazed Pears
2 tablespoons oil
4 firm pears, halved
Juice of 1 lemon
1 tablespoon honey

Serves 6–8

1 To make the Sweet Rice Pudding, preheat the oven to 300°F (150°C). Place the rice in a medium-sized heatproof bowl. Cover the rice with boiling water, allow to stand for 3 minutes, then drain. Place the rice into a medium-sized, heavy-bottomed saucepan. Add the milk, vanilla bean and sugar. Stir over low heat for 35 minutes. Remove the vanilla bean and stir in the cream. Transfer to a greased medium-sized heatproof dish and bake in the oven until the rice is tender, about 30 minutes.
2 To make the Grilled Honey Glazed Pears, preheat the grill or stovetop grill pan, then brush the grill surface with the oil. Combine the lemon juice and honey and brush the mixture onto the cut side of the pears. Grill the pear halves, cut side down until golden and slightly softened, about 2–3 minutes. Remove from the grill and serve immediately with the warm Sweet Rice Pudding.

Grilled Mangoes and Peaches with Raspberry Coulis

This pretty combination of sun-colored peaches and mango and vibrant red coulis captures the essence of summer. If you are making this grilled dessert when peaches or rapsberries aren't in season, simply omit the peaches (it's much easier to find good mangoes year-round) and use frozen raspberries.

2 mangoes
1 peaches
2 tablespoons oil

Raspberry Coulis
2 cups (1 pint/300 g) fresh or frozen raspberries (thawed if frozen)
Juice of 1 orange
2 tablespoons powdered sugar

Serves 6–8

1 To make the Raspberry Coulis, place the raspberries, orange juice and sugar into a food processor and process until smooth. Refrigerate before serving.
2 Cut the fleshy cheeks from the mango and discard the seed. Cut the peaches in half and carefully remove the seeds. Preheat a grill or stovetop grill pan, then brush the grill surface with the oil. Grill the fruit until golden, about 1 minute each side. Remove from the grill and serve warm or chilled with the Raspberry Coulis.

Published by Periplus Editions, Ltd., with editorial
offices at 61 Tai Seng Avenue, #02-12, Singapore
534167.

Hardcover ISBN 13: 978-0-7946-5040-7
          ISBN 10: 0-7946-5040-6
Printed in Singapore

Distributed by
USA
Tuttle Publishing, 364 Innovation Drive,
North Clarendon, VT 05759-9436.
Tel: (802) 773-8930 Fax: (802) 773-6993
info@tuttlepublishing.com
www.tuttlepublishing.com

Asia Pacific
Berkeley Books Pte Ltd.
61 Tai Seng Avenue
#02-12, Singapore 534167.
Tel: (65) 6280-1330 Fax: (65) 6280-6290
inquiries@periplus.com.sg
www.periplus.com

10 09 08   5 4 3 2 1